The Class Vote

Bill Aree

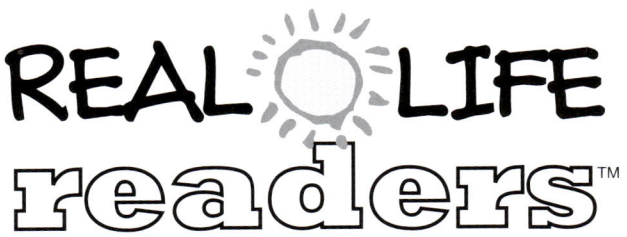

New York

This is our class.

Today we are having a party.

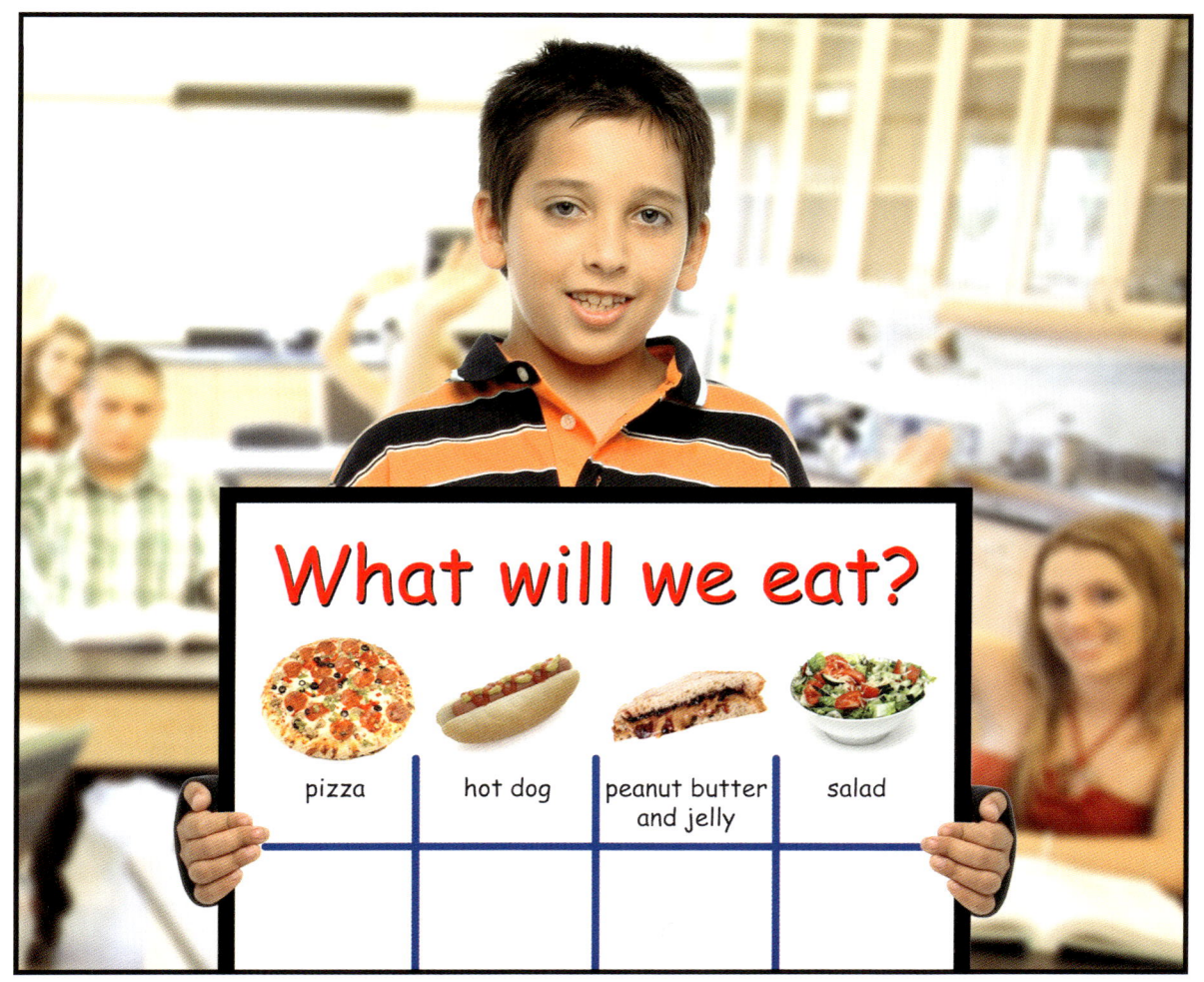

We will pick a food to eat at the party.
Here are some foods that we like.

How will we pick?
We will **vote** for the food we like.

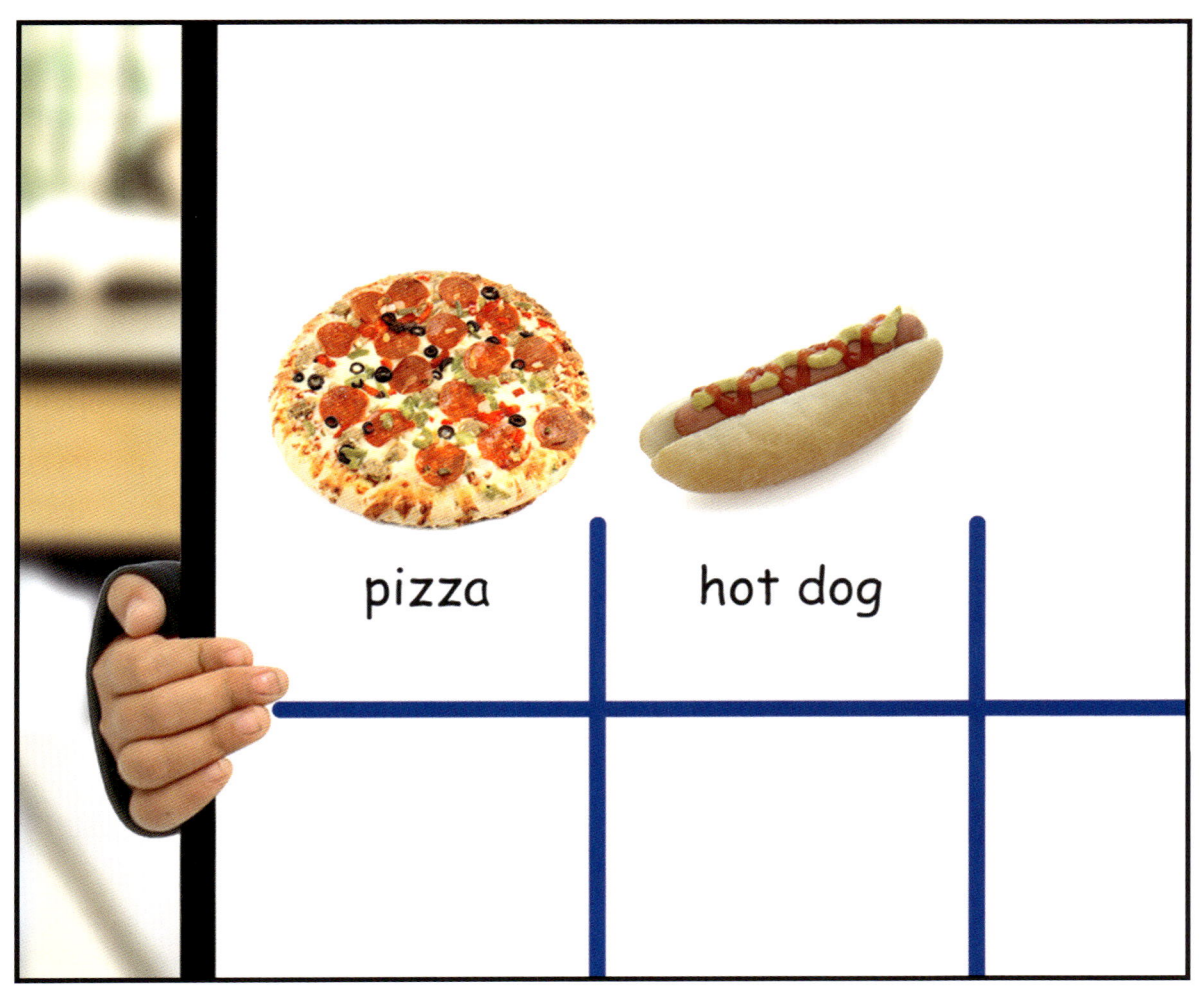

Will we eat pizza
or hot dogs?

Will we eat **peanut butter** and jelly or **salad**?

We will vote for the food that we want to eat.

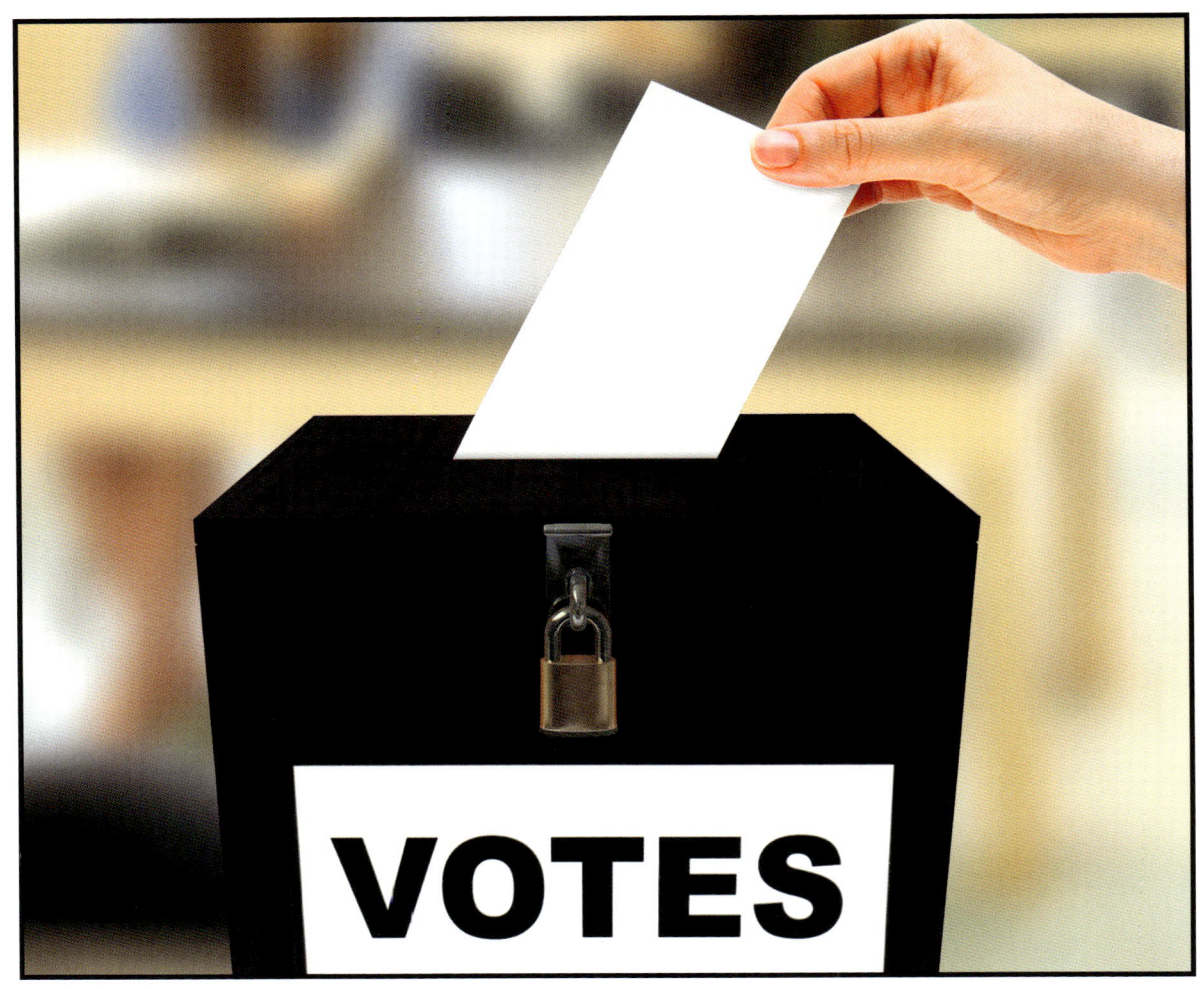

Now we vote.
We will eat the food that gets the most votes.

We count the votes.

We mark them on the **chart**.

More people voted for pizza.

We eat pizza at our party!

We like pizza!

The Class Vote

Each person votes for one food.

↓

We count the votes.

↓

We eat the food that gets the most votes.

Glossary

chart A large paper used to sort written facts.

peanut butter A spread made from peanuts.

salad A mix of raw vegetables.

vote To tell or show which one you would like.